The National Poetry Series established the Robert Fagles Translation Prize in 2007. This award is given to a translator who has shown exceptional skill in the translation of contemporary international poetry into English.

The Robert Fagles Translation Prize

2010
Eléna Rivera, *The Rest of the Voyage*
a translation of French poet Bernard Noël

2008
Lawrence Venuti, *Edward Hopper*
a translation of Catalan poet Ernest Farrés

2007
Marilyn Hacker, *King of a Hundred Horsemen*
a translation of French poet Marie Étienne

The National Poetry Series was established in 1978 to ensure the publication of poetry books annually through participating publishers. Publication is funded by the Lannan Foundation; Stephen Graham; Joyce & Seward Johnson Foundation; Glenn and Renee Schaeffer; Juliet Lea Hillman Simonds Foundation; Tiny Tiger Foundation; and Charles B. Wright III.

THE REST OF THE VOYAGE

Other Books by Bernard Noël (partial list)

In French:

L'Outrage aux mots: Œuvres II, P.O.L., 2011
Les Plumes d'Éros: Œuvres I, P.O.L., 2010
Un trajet en hiver, P.O.L., 2004
Romans d'un regard, P.O.L., 2003
La Face de silence, P.O.L, 2002
La Maladie du sens, P.O.L., 2001
Le roman d'Adam et Eve, L'Atelier des Brisants, 2001
Le Reste du voyage, P.O.L. 1997; Reissue, Points/poésie Seuil, 2006
La Chute des temps, Flammarion, 1983; reissue Gallimard, 1993
L'Ombre du double: poèmes, P.O.L., 1993
Les Premiers mots, Flammarion, 1973, reissue 1990
Le Syndrome de Gramsci: roman, P.O.L., 1993
Le Château de Cène, reissue Gallimard, 1992
Journal du regard, P.O.L., 1988, republished by 1994
Dictionaire de la commune, Hazan, 1971;
reissue Champs/Flammarion, 2 vol., 1977
Extraits du corps, Minuit, 1958; reissue Poésie/Gallimard, 2006

In English:

The Castle of Communion (le Château de Cène), Atlas Press, 1993
Time-Fall (la Chute des temps), Editions VVV Editions, 2006

Other Books by Eléna Rivera

The Perforated Map, Shearsman Books, 2011
Remembrance of Things Plastic, LRL e-editions, 2010
Secret of Breath by Isabelle Baladine Howald (trans. Eléna Rivera),
Burning Deck, 2008
In Respect of Distance, Beard of Bees, 2007
Mistakes, Accidents and a Want of Liberty, Barque Press, 2006
Suggestions at Every Turn, Seeing Eye Books (now Mindmade Books), 2005
Unknowne Land, Kelsey Street, 2000

THE REST OF THE VOYAGE

Poems

BERNARD NOËL

Translated from the French by Eléna Rivera

Graywolf Press

This publication is made possible in part by a grant provided by the
Minnesota State Arts Board, through an appropriation by the Minnesota
State Legislature from the Minnesota arts and cultural heritage fund with
money from the vote of the people of Minnesota on November 4, 2008, and
a grant from the Wells Fargo Foundation Minnesota. Significant support
has also been provided by the National Endowment for the Arts; Target;
the McKnight Foundation; and other generous contributions from
foundations, corporations, and individuals. To these organizations
and individuals we offer our heartfelt thanks.

Le Reste du voyage was first published by Editions P.O.L., Paris, France, 1997.

Published by Graywolf Press
250 Third Avenue North, Suite 600
Minneapolis, Minnesota 55401

www.graywolfpress.org

Published in the United States of America

ISBN 978-1-55597-600-2

2 4 6 8 9 7 5 3 1
First Graywolf Printing, 2011

Library of Congress Control Number: 2011930488

Cover design: Kyle G. Hunter

Cover art: Keith Waldrop, *Voyage*

CONTENTS

PREFACE

Eléna Rivera's translation of Bernard Noël's *Le Reste du voyage/The Rest of the Voyage* is at once original and remarkably faithful—indeed, its originality lies in the care and music the translator has brought to her commitment to follow Noël's forms as closely as possible. *Le Reste du voyage,* despite its fluid and immediate tone, is a book of strict formal order: it consists of 111 pages built from groups of eleven-syllable lines. In observing this principle of set form and syllabic verse, Rivera succeeds beautifully in setting the rhythms of the French original into English. If we are more familiar with the residue of Anglo-Saxon common meters in English poetry, this translation reminds us of the thread of Latin and Romance languages in general and the hendecasyllabic line in particular that, as well, underlie our tradition. The succession of poems has a fluency that becomes as mesmerizing as any mode of transport, for Rivera is remarkably adept at varying the lines, landing with emphasis or muting the effect as she follows the speed and light of Noël's themes.

Those themes are no less than a meditation on the traveler's encounter with landscape in the late twentieth century. The book is constructed in three parts: a long opening poem narrating the speaker's pilgrimage to Mount Athos—the remote holy mountain, which only men may visit, of the Greek Orthodox faith; a center section made up of one-page poems based on the experience of viewing a series of individual sites at varying speeds; and a final section, a single meditation on language, made up of thirty-three short sections. Noël takes on distant shots and close-ups, moving too quickly to see particulars or so slowly that objects become abstractions, conveying the smells, tastes, and sounds of each location in wholes and parts, reflexively considering what is invisible to a visitor, and meditating on the ancient theme of the voyage of life with great vividness and freshness. The work is thus a topographical poem, but one of Dantean intensity as the poet explores the limits of knowledge in changing circumstances of observation. In the end, the question of conversion is answered by motion itself, for here to view is to review, to visit is to revisit.

Born in 1930 in Aveyron, Bernard Noël is one of the most distinguished living writers in France; he has won the Prix National de Poésie and the Grand Prix International Guillevic-Ville de Saint-Malo for his poetry, and he is celebrated as well as an art critic and as the author of a number of daring, often erotic, novels of implicit social criticism. In France his work is published by the prestigious houses of Gallimard, Seuil, P.O.L., and Minuit, and he has been translated into nine languages. Yet Rivera's is the first translation of his poetry into English, and her work thus remedies an unfortunate weakness in English-language letters.

SUSAN STEWART

INTRODUCTION

*Le corps est une carrière à mots et ses explorateurs assurent que là,
sous la peau, il y a de quoi refaire la langue.*

BERNARD NOËL

Bernard Noël was born in 1930 at Sainte-Geneviève-sur-Argence, in
the Aveyron region in the Midi-Pyrénées in southern France. At fifteen,
in Catholic school, he described having an "experience of God," which
prompted his leaving the Church as well as changing his first name, his
school, and his future. Some of his early literary influences were Malcolm
Lowry and Faulkner, as well as Choderlos de Laclos, Mallarmé, Nerval,
Blanchot, Bataille, Rimbaud, and Artaud among others. He wrote his
first book of poems during his military service which he bore badly. He
was, like many of his generation in France, marked by the dropping of
the atomic bomb, the discovery of concentration camps, the crimes of
Stalin, the wars in Indochina, Korea, and especially Algeria. His first
book *Les Yeux chimères* was published in 1955, and in 1958 the prose
poems *Extraits du corps,* after which there was a long silence when he
didn't write for over ten years.

In the early 1960s, Nöel was part of a support network for Algerian
militants of the FNL then in a struggle for independence from France
during the Algerian War. In December 1961, he was arrested with an
Algerian who had just handed him some documents that he was to take
abroad. They were able to conceal the documents in a bench at a café be-
fore the police arrested them. He was held for three weeks in a cell of
the Dépôt, a detention center that had been used by the Gestapo during

the war, and the Algerian was tortured. This incident, and his horror of the hypocrisy and bad faith that pervaded that period in France, dampened his ambition to be a writer and he stopped writing for ten years.

His silence was broken when he published his next book, *La Face de silence* (*The Face of Silence*, 1967), and later the controversial *Le Château de Cène* (*Castle of Communion*, 1969), a work of erotic fiction, which he said liberated him from an internal censure. He originally published *Le Château de Cène* under a pseudonym, but later republished it under his own name. The book was banned for obscenity in 1973 and Noël was put on trial for *"outrage aux bonnes moeurs,"* the last trial of its kind in France. Around the same time, in 1968, he worked on the *Dictionnaire de la Commune* (published in 1971), finding that the only way to write about history was to write it as a dictionary.

After 1969, he wrote poetry, novels, plays, essays, and became noted as an influential art critic, writing on such artists as Magritte, Matisse, André Masson, Olivier Debré, Viera da Silva, Henri Michaux, and Zao Wou-Ki. He has since then published over forty books in different genres, and the first volume of his collected works, *Les Plumes d'Éros: Œuvres I,* was published by P.O.L. in 2010. He has won numerous awards including the Grand Prix National de Poésie in 1993.

The Rest of the Voyage (originally published in 1997 and then republished in 2006) is divided into three sections. The first, "Passing Mount Athos," recounts Noël's visit to Mount Athos, in Greece, to one of the Eastern Orthodox monasteries. Describing the rituals, the antiquities, the remains of previous inhabitants, he explores themes of the body, mortality, language, and the gaze—how the seen is changed by the seeing and then articulated. Noël spent a month in the company of four monks living at Saint-André (only men are allowed entrance to Mount Athos), going to their services, working with them and taking down notes in his notebook. Though not a believer, he saw that he could share the rituals with the monks without sharing their *raison d'être.* In an interview, Noël describes the monastic rituals as "metrical," how the monastic rhythm can be applied to a whole other "container." The notes he kept in his notebook looked "vertical," verse-like in appearance, but they didn't have the condensation of verse, so he decided to give each line an "armature," rewriting his notes into hendecasyllable lines. He was interested in the eleven-syllable line because in French it is considered asymmetric, awkward, nonpoetical, which was in keeping with his passion for the *"défi de l'impair!"* (challenge of the irregular!")

Even before Noël informed me that the whole book was written in eleven-syllable lines, I was aware of a very definite rhythm. The lines, characteristically unpunctuated, stand alone, and at the same time skillfully utilize enjambment to keep the poem moving forward—not just moving forward, but shifting the sense of the poem slightly. His lines are elusive because of this, constantly changing, able to be read in various syntactical permutations according to what comes before and what comes after, keeping the reader attentive to the line itself. When he informed me that the book was written in hendecasyllabic lines, he explained that in French poetry the eleven-syllable line had always been considered *"boiteux,"* ("cumbersome" or "clumsy"). French poetry up to the twentieth century was mostly written in eight-, ten-, or twelve-syllable lines, but mostly in the twelve-syllable alexandrine. In English prosody we don't regularly count syllables, we count beats, for example in the five stresses of the iambic pentameter line, but eleven syllables seemed strange enough in English to warrant the engagement. The hendecasyllable was first used by Sappho in what was later called the Sapphic Stanza; it was several centuries later employed by the Roman poet Catullus, and the form became as prevalent in Italian poetry as the alexandrine is in French poetry. For Noël, the hendecasyllable was *"Quelque chose qui soit très contraignant et invisible comme une règle monastique."* ("Something that would be a strong constraint and invisible like a monastic rule.")

A translator cannot translate the untranslatable quality of another language, nor a particular language's meter (French and English being very different in this respect), but a translator can bring a poem to life in another language, make a poem take on the responsibility for the presence of the other poet's vision, their images, rhythm, sound. I became an interpreter *within* Noël's poems, as if the poems were growing out of an understanding, a closeness to the words. Counting syllables made me very attentive to the effort of combining sound, rhythm, images, and the "intellect" or "sense" of the poem; I worked very closely with the thesaurus, trying to find ways to lengthen a short line, to shorten a long line, while still staying true to the other elements of the poems. The eleven-syllable line curiously became the means for this meeting between languages. At first I thought I would never be able to work with such a constraint over a long book of poems, but it soon allowed me to let go of the French and make poems in English from his poems. In the movement from French to English, on that bridge, translation happened.

The second section of *The Rest of the Voyage* is comprised of forty-four single poems, impressions of cities, places, trains, where Noël, in his attention to the present, writes of the world and its diversity. In this section Noël worked directly in eleven syllables, without the use of notes, in "vertical" one-page poems that focus on geographical places, and the "seeing" that happens there. These short glimpses, "photographs," into place become a kind of mapping of our contemporary, ever-changing landscape, and explore how that landscape is altered by how we view it and by the language that we use to represent it. In these poems, Noël brings us closer, not just to the seen, but to what is unseen, invisible, buried; he rejects the easy associations that we have with certain places and our engagement with them. Here, for example, he writes poems where he examines a past that collides with the present and its ever-encroaching surfaces; he juxtaposes various notions of time, architecture, ideals, ideas of beauty, and the way that the old is idealized sometimes at the cost of the present; at the same time, he also writes about the ways the ancient is often undervalued, buried behind new facades, built upon, or completely destroyed. There are no easy solutions in his poetry; there is only seeing, the effort of seeing, seeing ourselves and what is around us, what is "other." Speed and technological changes have altered and multiplied the ways the world is viewed, both the personal and peripheral worlds.

The third section of the book was written in Mexico, in a notebook bought in New York. Noël revised a poem he was working on, changing it into five sections of 111 hendecasyllable lines. He didn't like the results, took out parts, rewrote others, and destroyed the rest. The result is thirty-three short poems (yet another variation on the number eleven), the remains, the "rest," of what was going to be a much longer work. In this last section, "The Rest of the Poem," he is present to experience, absence, nothingness, the body, mortality, language, history, and the role of "the mental," which he would say is the same as saying "the role of language." The voyage here references an inner physical space, the place/ space of the poem, here, now, in language. As he says in an interview, what he was looking for was a skeleton, a skeleton around which the words could become flesh, *"Toute oeuvre est ce qu'elle est . . . une empreinte."* ("All oeuvre is what it is . . . a trace.")

In the midst of chaos each instant is re-created by the gaze, by language. In all three sections, Noël writes of the ruins, the chaos around him, and the inevitable mortality that is part of human life. He does this without morbidity; he is instead amazed at the constructions, the images, that are present in his experience of time and place. Noël is interested in the effort that is needed to meet the world and others. His poems bring us to a heightened sense of attention, ready to explore the ever-changing behind the facades, behind the speed, behind the invented, so as to see and be attentive to what *is*. By doing so, brings the reader back to the present.

I originally began to translate *The Rest of the Voyage* when I was asked to translate a few poems for a new anthology of contemporary French poetry. I was surprised to learn that, though Noël's poems had been widely translated into many languages, only two of his books, a novel, *The Castle of Communion (Le Château de Cène),* and a book of poetry, *Time-Fall (La Chute des temps),* had been translated into English. Translating *The Rest of the Voyage* has been an incredible "voyage," both working with what was on the page, and reading from Noël's immense oeuvre. Translating Noël involved many layers of discovery, in language, in the body, in the self. Noël's range of interests, his intellectual acumen, his complete presence in the writing have made translating him an immense resource and gift.

Noël was about to turn eighty when I met him in 2010 for a reading we gave in Paris, organized by Double Change, an organization that curates a bilingual reading series in Paris, New York, and London. I had been working on this book off and on since 2005 and was now meeting him for the first time. I was not disappointed. Bernard Noël is a true gentleman, soft-spoken, generous, someone who is very present to what is right in front of him. He takes care with everyone he meets. He listens. In an interview with Jean-Luc Bayard, he says how he is not interested in thinking about the future. He is only interested in the present moment. *"La leçon numero un de l'écriture, c'est qu'elle est au présent. On ne peut écrire qu'au présent"* ("The number one lesson in writing, is that it takes place in the present. One can't write any other way but in the present"), he says in the interview. The tense may change, he says, but the writing is always done in the present. He later quotes Joyce, *"tout est: 'Work-in-progress' jusqu'au bout."*

Noël invited my husband and me to Mauregny where he now lives in a farmhouse filled with books, music, and artworks. He doesn't own a car, though he lives in the country. He makes jam, collects walnuts, reads, writes, walks a lot, travels a lot, and is continually in conversation with other writers and artists. He is deeply concerned with the commercialization of language and culture. If consuming becomes all, he asks, will culture become our lost paradise? He thinks it is important to distinguish the visible from the real. He is concerned with censure, both self-inflicted and inflicted by others for political or social reasons. He is extremely mindful of the ways that the media attempts to rob us of our experience, by co-opting our words and feeding us language and ideas. Noël is an observer, a traveler, a poet whose concerns are life itself, how the body lives life, and how the corporeality of *polis* presents itself, in all its permutations—the responsibility to the world around us and the people around us. Bernard Noël's poems bring the reader back to language, to the present moment, to looking, to seeing the ways we make the world around us in language, in the midst of our need for sustainability and true empathy toward others. *"Il faut faire un effort pour lire, pour regarder, pour aimer . . . il faut faire un effort vers l'Autre."* ("One must make an effort to read, to look, to love . . . one must make an effort toward the other.")

ELÉNA RIVERA

THE REST OF THE VOYAGE

PASSING MOUNT ATHOS

1.

a word seeks my heart and me around it I
search for how it grabs ahold of its present
a little of this thing that floats around here
everywhere devastation ruins and yet
only its lovely image is nipped by time
Saint John submerges his pen into the light
with steady gesture though the luminous stream
aims at one knows not what part of the body
here flies are going to forage in its dust
then fly away toward the *cul-de-four* where God
has blackened so much that he is negative
the eagle and John same halo just one wing
to Mark's lion the eye a small pool of tears
Luke's face has been eaten away by mildew
he has become a black man with a white beard
no more Matthew just a hole in the mortar
and a few bones in pinkish rose a hornet
pulls my gaze toward the dome up there somewhere in
the first circle the remains of a shoulder
in the second eight angels with six wings two
toward the bottom two toward the top two open
the whole is the height of sensuality
each angel appears two times provided for
in a zone that's evenly split human beings
have only one time and love would be to make
in an embracing of the high and the low
circular and without end a wheel always
in motion and the same hornet descends toward
the flow of lava fresh bird droppings my eye
inflamed all the same not daring to use it
but I confuse perhaps bird droppings and gall
and there I am in the middle of this day
my gaze all of a sudden cracked by the sun
emptiness and fear of the rotten staircase

eyes feel for the air on their left then the brusque
surprise arises
                    the White the White the White
pushes deep into sky its chalk erection
life death and reality on top of it
put up a tremendous NO to their reasons

2.

no flesh up there with the angels with six wings
their sensuality grows in this nothing
but to have it off in air for a halo
isn't it a fair virtual war me who these
days hasn't had more sex than little Jesus
I listen to words in Greek in the distance
bubbles of sound the same as these mysteries
that roll in the space and produce in the ear
farting sounds and there are more and more flies than
yesterday but the pigeons added nothing
I came to see the White
                            its peak is topped with
a milky-white pyramid this the only
cloud in sight in all the cottony sky that
covers thus the violence of duration

3.

the image and the word are they linked or else
always one after the other prevailing
each in its own good time to see or to say
what the eyes have seen over there but being
seen isn't enough it sets itself up prowls
lashes out against the movement of the poem
but what is a surge of mineral and white
a vertical silence a period of stone

4.

tear it from my eyes make something else of it
I told myself while climbing the marble stairs
which overlook the emptiness then I walk
on the ridge of a wall then on some old planks
worn away by the rain the sun and this time
I know where to find it of course it is there
but all gray in the blue mist the wood cracks snaps
under my weight or from the torrents of light

5.

sitting in the freshness of ruins I see
John's pen take some air in the same way language
does but mine doesn't it turns in vain a bit
of breath doesn't draw from it the needed form
there a last bit of plaster falls from the dome
and creates a lot of dust with what there was
a page at my hand similar why am I
touched by the intact by the implacable
youthfulness here in these four marble columns
their skins so diaphanous under the sun
their curves so insolent these sirens of stone

6.

very ordinary morning a peak flanked
by a double slope that serves as horizon
a discolored saint in its corner and me
looking at the sky a slight wind underlines
the silence to the left a ruined building
the fire has baked the stones wrung the iron
the ashes that we see would be that of books

7.

words could easily give up lots of things like
fingers of the dead don't need to be useful
thunder in the distance moves bunch of empty
crates the four yew trees at the fountain point to
the direction of the motionless the earth
rotates without crying the air just a round
blue eddy in the thickness of who knows what

8.

under the floor of *osteophylakion*
the bones mix in a way those bodies never
did at the left when entering sixty-one
skulls on nine counters all without lower jaws
so the teeth appear under each of them like
little footsteps on the wall at the far back
the ten countertops of the large crânothèque
three rows on each of the sixty and fifteen
say around two hundred and twenty that one
needs to multiply by ten just one blackish
date on its forehead of nineteen thirty-five
nineteen thirty-eight is displayed to the right
and its neighbor nineteen forty-one proclaims
the other to the left all the frontal bone
that bear the Russian line and three that espouse
rotundity are holding on to the name
as well as perhaps the monastic rank there
always there's a black cross between the arcades
or rather they're traced at the sutures of three
cranial bones how to take in hand a skull
other than two fingers pinching the orbits
that very fine septum that cracks or gets crushed
many are so white that I forget the dust

one can also handle them thumb and index
spread wide apart by the temples or cheekbones
on top of the front ledge of the main window
two or three dozen are covered in spider
webs to a large doornail a little further
a few instruments of torture iron hats
crosses one locked around the throat and you have
to be two to take hold of it to lift it
these led cinctures and shackles of every kind
there on a table and inside wood boxes
are these skulls that probably were once precious
nineteen hundred and seven on a yellow
forehead and nineteen hundred and twenty-three
between green temples and a pile of hundreds
of tibias white logs stacked in a corner

9.

it has disappeared into the clouds unless
a thunderbolt didn't decapitate it
when I die the entire world dies with me
said father Maximos we were discussing
grace I answered that it seemed to me that it's
fundamental in the Orient whereas
Rome was constructed on power Maximos
celebrates the three daily offices at
six seven and nine I like how he's able
to handle the thurible with twelve small bells
one for each apostle and makes us a path
of smoke I also like how he psalmodies
Kyrie Jesou Chistou Yié tou Theou
eleison imas our Lord Jesus Christ
son of God have pity on us I counted
up to seventy-seven times this morning
eighty-three times yesterday at the evening

office this appeal dates to its beginnings
with the hermetic life of Saint Anthony
chanted while facing demons Saint Gregory
Palamas introduced it at Mount Athos
where we are a very small community
the father Paul and the abbot Maximos
his brother Estaphios diminutive
Staphy (which I took for daddy while smiling
believing my two monks daddyfying their
father) are the three permanent of our skete
built for eight hundred Russian monks then and was
a bastion of the empire of the last tsar
only thing Greek here is the chapel where I
go by the top of a wall wooden staircase
it was dated they said in the seventeenth
the provisionary members of our skete
are apart from me Niko a young student
in theology father Dimitrios
who weighs as much on his own as the other
three fault of his generous twofold stomach
that earned him a good heart

10.

the nearby ruins
make a stone coffin of their own remainders
the gaze buries itself then looks back around
hoping to grab hold of the thing that threatens
and which is however nowhere a rusting
of air an eczema on the skin of day
a bird dives toward the cat brushing against him
again and again to the life to the death

11.

how much time is necessary for time to
wear away a closed community one gave
the name of future to the capacity
of giving up one's place to the next as if
those that were here before didn't have future
except the one that each had his own small life
the Russian Revolution having cut short
succession which is where the thought of man goes
conscious that there will be no survivors
to live therefore is an exercise in death
while dying is day after day the only
point in common and then comes the end of time
for the very last one the one that collapsed
all alone dry in his black habit and me
behind more than a thousand doors I look for
a cadaver for the last dead

12.

                    attracted
by something and that something is the wait that
I have my desire thrown into absence
making traces of a name tremble this name
carried out in me the work that carried out
in air a silent pitter-patter of wings

13.

Mondays and Wednesdays and Fridays are fast days
during lunchtime there's two or three tomatoes
just as much in the evening other days a
large plate with vegetable or pasta lots
of bread spring water and sometimes even fish

or feta yogurt with honey little sleep
they're taking a nap me I listen to time
that passes like a breath

14.

                    it is there massive
and dark but decapitated of its peak
by a flat ivory cloud we did not fast
at lunchtime because what Paul told me is that
today is the feast of the twelve apostles
which gives us right to oil Demétrios
therefore prepared some pasta in a red sauce
I write in the little Greek chapel Saint John
doesn't ever tire of dipping his pen
the four curvaceous ones are always so svelte
the small cross-arch above displays two angels
and a holy knight a cross in his right hand
a sword in the left and two cartouches with
sepia landscapes further a flowering
arc frames an angel that would do just as well
as young damsel than young squire its right hand
picks a tune on the lyre on its left wing
more rubble than yesterday art decreases
every day it will eventually seep from
walls like this image oozed from the body that
one sees in the linen of the shroud

15.

                        must one
mustn't one lend to the shadows a little
bit of life not just to those under the earth
doing their job of being dead but to those
that double the things from a bottom so deep

that here we still think walking in the middle
of one's own body the ground then seems to be
the jaw that's missing at the base of the skulls

16.

Father Paul's narrative: The large church was inaugu-
rated in 1901. There was a lot of talk in Athos because
the church seemed so unseemly and impertinent. Greek
and Byzantine tradition is not at all about these grand
imperial machines. The monastic buildings had been
completed for a number of years. They sheltered eight
hundred monks. You see these immense buildings;
they form a large square that stretches out around the
church. Seen from the outside, with their thick bases,
they look like fortresses. At the end of the last century,
the Russians tried to establish themselves everywhere,
here, in Lebanon, in Palestine, under the guise of reli-
gious foundations. We found millions of guns in the
caves, and under the buildings, way over there, there
was a cartridge factory. Maybe the monks didn't know
anything about it, they weren't soldiers but the lead-
ership was religious and political. Then a sacrilege oc-
curred that led to the repatriation of half of the monks
in 1912. Three boats came to fetch them. Afterwards,
new monks replaced them, but war came, then there
was revolution soon after, and the young went off to
fight on the side of the Whites. There remained four
hundred or so monks at the start of the twenties; they
began to grow old without young people coming to re-
place them. They say that at the end, there was a fu-
neral every day. The abbot was the last one, in 1960,
and then only a single monk remained, the only Greek
monk of the monastery who served as secretary and in-
terpreter. This Greek monk began to sell everything,

putting the finishing touches to the work of the great
fire of 1958, which destroyed the heart of this house by
burning the library and treasure . . .

17.

wave after wave go from the sea to the sky
the mountains and highest of them all the White
pretends again one day to be another
in the middle of milky gray emulsion
pine, fig tree, green oak and every now and then
a few monastic houses and all of this
perfect for the blue hinterland just inland
it ripples down below and groans on the rocks
breaks through some sun it covers itself with scales
making a silver hem on the horizon
I didn't know that the sea was also here
all these days having taken it for low sky
but there is no doubt of its identity
from Stravronikita fortified castle
overhanging and crowned with these high walls and
apartments balconies courtyard with arcades
Turkish delights glass of water for new guests
to go to heaven with starting from the church
it's enough to know how to climb the ladder
but warning to the one who falls he goes straight
in between Leviathan's jaws saintly crowd
of martyrs one of them has their hands chopped off
then feet the human body has too many
extremities each provide such temptation
for the hangmen an icon in mosaic
of Saint Nicholas was pulled out from the sea
in a net from the ancient times it had on
its forehead an oyster when it was torn off
the wound that it covered then started to bleed
the wound is still there

18.

sometimes hands hold tightly
a piece of memory they have not taken
it is there on their skin having come back since
the substance of flesh is dense unless a heart
starts to flow suddenly in another heart

19.

day puts shades in the hollow of the orbits
the smell of silence very cold a closet
gives shelter to a largish crown of lilies
white roses and forget-me-nots above it
a skull from nineteen hundred and one and next
in a glass closet in a pyramid shape
three skulls highest one dead in eighteen hundred
and seventy-one while the one on the left
died only in nineteen hundred thirty-four
the other on its head a blank black label
behind the pane of glass at the lowest part
there are three shelves and on each one are ten skulls
one from nineteen hundred and six displaying
six lines of mystery and a cross made of
four black triangles makes one think of holding
in one's hands very large fragile empty eggs
beneath the hatch angle of the *skullothèque*
it is not at all what I had imagined
nothing but disordered stacks a scrap of bones
broken ribs in a cold draughty air current
in one of the gloomy annexed rooms there are
two tables loaded with neatly ordered skulls
large insects incrusted in white one senses
them prepared to throw themselves forward the most
lively have already climbed on the others

20.

it's two thousand and thirty meters a bit
less than Olympus assures Maximos but
more than Parnassus a large cloud looms over
the wind stirs the air rolls over the shoulder
of stones no other human noise a softness
oozes from the ruins marjoram bushes
and a well-known wise man lives very near here
students pay him a visit and then demand
a miracle he goes into his kitchen
and takes a large knife I will cut off your head
he says then you will put it back on and make
a distinctive sign so there's no question of
error each of the students declined to act
and so the monk concluded: not one of you
is ready for the miracle

21.

            a young horse
demonstrated in passing the true meaning
of the word "high-spirited" but how is the
sign of use to me when I don't have the horse

22.

to pin together impressions one by one
I try on words but what is an impression
which is not able then to coincide with
the tongue makes no progress with the heart the head
the impression lies on the throat and presses
but who could use up all the air that they breathe

23.

very romantic this morning it is dark
against a blue sail and wearing a hat like
the one Fracasse wore at right an arabesque
drives the sky ruthlessly the rest is startled
by daybreak the sweat of the silence and no
chirruping of sparrows or of the windswept
chaos one would have to sit this specific
morning out on all things the sun already
takes up the whole of the room and stings the eyes

24.

in gray rubble trail the wings of an angel
a star and some grapes made of plaster a Christ
arms lifted for the crucifixion a horse
broken in two parts a head with punctured eyes
we walk on the tip of our toes wondering
why there's all this clamor all these *coups de grâce*
for some objects one venerated right here
the ceiling is on the wooden floor the floor
bends under footsteps floorboards eaten by rain
on a bed of blue wood an open closet
three chubby ones without trumpets and the dead
leaves near the door two necks smashed in the eagle
of Byzantium was usurped by the tsar

25.

the church a celestial warehouse with five naves
some seepage but apart from that in good shape
all the iconostasis' gold intact
as well as its hundred or so figures two
gigantic chandeliers under the dome and

beneath the keystone of the great nave banners
icons painted with gold backgrounds some paintings
where pass a pre-Raphaelite impression
an example a Christ on the cross flanked by
the Virgin John all surrounded by white wings
whose beautiful movements weave inside the gaze
and keep it dancing until it notices
three angels with very feminine hairstyles
set down in a large red sky with moon and clouds
treated flatly the way Gauguin might have done
all the feminine is angelical here
the heads attached where the wings articulate
drifting in pairs on the slight breeze of pink air
or gray while taking on the postures of swans
up on top immense tribunal where one gets
to a room with a closet and five bodies
that had probably sheltered chasubles by
the dozens it contains nothing but coat racks
but they're worthy of a folk art museum
a golden plinth two tabernacles and one
broom that's placed on a beautiful envelope
with three photographer angels in relief
one manipulating the gadget's bellows
the other occupied in developing
the third in midst of admiring a cliché
a flap that reads Paul Sebah photographer
four hundred thirty-nine high-street of Pera
Cairo on the Esbekieb then above
an empty escutcheon one guesses the word
Paris in the envelope man with moustache
big shoulder epaulettes decorations and
orders' sash
                    behind the iconostasis
the altar under a canopy of white
marble that contains columns of gray marble
red tablecloth book covered in violet

velvet but the most remarkable is at
the wall the tomb of the Resurrection that
blows blazing white fire in the direction
of terrified soldiers all piled and crammed in

26.

seated in front of a Christ in glory same
as Peter the Great suddenly swept by grace
instead of a drink a gesture of blessing
luminous leader throne at the clouds' summit
when the Verb makes itself image who is that
further on two panels are arranged the Twelve
all of the space here proclaims their victory
and their message it's that which they imagine
in Christ's glory seen everywhere positions
taken forever fixed in the one meaning
one has to stand separate from the species
to become a disseminator of faith

27.

go to the fountain to procure fresh water
and encounter a pile of hazelnut shells
the thought of the squirrel chases for a moment
the thought of the unthinkable

28.

                    what's the good
of all these walls these collections of carved rocks
throughout the world in the form of truth if not
to turn away from the coming of nothing
whole massive order constructed against it

for protection in which each one can ignore
the void while being gratified by some thing
celestial or philosophic occupant
evil sin are worth more than anxiety
in front of nothing this outrageous nothing
that astounds to such a point head and language
that their activities are now suspended
and thinking cannot make from this more thinking
this incapacity annihilates

29.

       thick
tablecloth of heat and vertical we go
under its escarpment wearing shoes of stone
the sheet metal on the roofing burps up fire
It is just barely a shadow in the mist
pigeons have come back to shit on the flagstones
in a foursquare made of square ceramic tiles
white marble rhombus carries at the center
the two-headed eagle seven feathered tail
one thousand seven hundred sixty-six is
this the date of the chapel a beak tapping
making a noise like drops of falling water

30.

cubicle chosen for its difficulty
no access the lintel collapsed on the door
one has to push aside the doorframe and slide
two swallows brush against my face and go out
with a cry into the milky horizon
their nest on the ceiling has a bizarre shape
a flattened vase the neck serving as entrance
a writing case nose to the ground a buffet

with hanging doors a lot of rubble and a
Russian style burning stove which I took at first
for an altar large balcony with a view
on the sea that for now merges with the sky
basin iron bedstead window scraps the yews
of the cemetery puncture the big blue
to the right without warning the White appears
abrupt peak presence in vibrant majesty

31.

no body would know how to cut its own breath
except in an act like Mallarmé's the one
he did with his glottis and doing the same
thought asphyxiates in the unthinkable
I never separated body and thought
the strangling of one is that of the other
the leap into death madness or ecstasy
excesses that deliver us from reason
otherwise said the transforming of being
into Necessity under ruins or
above I learn that a certain religious
state has you tear everything from its hinges
starting with words at the order of language
or of knowledge leave it to dance at the head
of a horse and this beyond good and evil
the God of the Bible is not reasonable
he set reason down inside a tree and said
that the fruits of it were lethal what labor
then to be able to put faith in reason
confuse heresy and frenzy colonize
mysterious pounding keep life pulsating
faith nevertheless must topple the mountains
overturn meanings of words of history
be this madness that drives out the evidence

the certainties that elect the disorder
erase then the consumption of the apple
the choice and the consequences
                                        the poem
instigates in the language the same madness
how could I have ever thought it otherwise
it wants its clarity to be rather wild
to tear at the heart and the skin of the eyes

32.

the great bear scurries over the library
Venus flits around on the top of a yew
the moon plays the game of the frog and the ox
with a cupola it's four meters by three
meters the dimensions of my cubicle
a blue door and an iron bedstead with board
a straw mattress and the window so deep that
it serves as a shelf for the laundry and books
I retrieved a chair and a little table
in the ruins

33.

            the accurate word comforts
and even appeases I don't know the names
of the three trees with pale flowers in front of
the entrance of the Grande Lavra what would I
know more by knowing them it would fix beauty
which in exchange would embellish it with a
precise image in that it would accomplish
an exact encounter between word and thing

still it has been days and days that I chew on
these words without drawing from them the least juice
makes sense the words ruins destruction rubble
that generally serve to close the matter
but in its presence no longer sufficient
as if accuracy could uncover here
the abyss into which it propels itself

34.

that we can say it and not think it replies
Aristotle to all his critics of the
essential principle of contradiction
how would he have retorted to the conduct
of a thing taking exception to its name
I know that an event a situation
is not in the word that categorizes
but the description which this word engages
no other point would know how to express space
nonetheless each one of them makes it exist

35.

the door opens onto some broken floorboards
three steps forward and the rubble starts cracking
rusted boxes the remains of a basin
on the left an iron bedstead a closet
at right drawers ripped out opposite a ghost
of a sideboard with glass paneling smashed in
an armful of dead branches and a pile of
leaves piled high underneath the missing window

36.

the door opens onto a gray partition
where some seedlings are aligned in blue patches
on the ground there is a large plaster seedbed
and bits of brick white and rose at the window
three fig branches have broken the windowpanes

37.

the door opens onto an enormous room
spiked with iron bedsteads rotten wooden floors
large rusted can pile of horsehair and stuffing
covers slashed and ripped to shreds armchair broken
nine accounting notebooks soiled by mortar
some metal boxes eaten into by rust
a teakettle studded with pieces of glass
a closet where the remains of a coat hang
three broken sideboards some cruets three basins
a handle made of porcelain four drawers
the right side of the room is thoroughly minced
all scrap iron and plaster and moldy boards

38.

the door opens onto an iron platter
a tangle of rags a broom without handle
a wooden cylinder with a metal band
three rusted round iron boxes a sideboard
a skillet a leather bag a writing case
a hammer an iron bedstead with its plank
where one half of Jerusalem trails beneath
the feet of the one Crucified with three scenes
of torture with cross in X thrusts of a sword
hanging head at bottom and flight of arrows

39.

the door fell sideways across the corridor
there's free access to this unrewarding view
piles of plaster broken boxes block wooden
slivers carpet beater a portable stove
in leather enameled bowls coin pocketbook
string intertwined all around a bit of board
sideboard without drawers plate filled with dozen
rusted keys corner cabinet with basin
triangulated zinc fountain of the same
and soapdish at the bottom of the window
two beautiful bottles in blown glass not one
centimeter of the floor that hasn't been
littered with objects as varied as cruets
the box springs of a bedstead enamel plates
scraps of fabric rusted nails tiny pieces
of metal wood paper brick and porcelain

40.

the inventory isolates separates
divides emits a contagious cleanliness
the word purifies the object of itself
cleanses it of its nature of disaster
it's just as exact as discouragingly
inexact and grateful to it always it
disappears the rubbish and shitty manure
the mortal juices where all of these things soak
there unless the gaze hasn't yet absorbed them

41.

the poem doesn't give a damn for fairness
the circle's radius or that two plus two
make fatally four besides it's the only
personal space where law becomes demented
eats the irrevocable returns to death
it's just as much itself than beside itself
became breath at the head and verbal vapor
phoenix of air always nascent on some lips

42.

no human has taste for the impossible
if one finds one that does they're feeble-minded
says Aristotle before him as after
say all the reasonable philosophers
all of which are large consumers of apples
and of enlightenment

43.

                    the door opens on
a dresser made of sheet metal iron box
a wooden footstool some shards of window-glass
rusted boxes a large slow-combustion stove
rising straight up to the ceiling hearth open
there's the library a mortar of ashes
where all that remains is a leather binding
mute and empty an iron bedstead and plank
spreading a palette a bit of vestment stole
with an embroidered cross strings brimming over
two very dry tubes that had some blue some red
a key a comb made of horn and three buttons
this cubicle overlooks a balcony
and the floor is nothing but minced bits of wood

44.

the doorway was forced open the large chapel
with blue walls when the plaster did not collapse
decay everywhere flooring torn pierced with holes
moldy fissures and balustrade in tatters
the iconostasis reduced to framework
seems as if it frames a void or an absence
virgin in corner at knees of an angel
cicadas and the sky pours into the sea

45.

the White isn't white owing to the whiteness
of the rock but by light's evaporation
strange consequence no doubt a coincidence
which then impacted my first glimpse of Athos
it is a pyramid between two shoulders
this morning and it exhales a bit of gray

46.

generators devastate the beginning
of the night but the annoyance doesn't last
we go to bed early or read with a lamp
noise and grease notwithstanding here is the most
well-preserved countryside in the world it's closed
no roads to the exterior one has to
first equip oneself with authorization
delivered by the provincial ministry
seen by this one or that one then you're allowed
to go to the port of Ouranoupoli
a Diamonitirion or Stamped Letter
from the Surveillance Sacrée (that is three stamps
two thousand drachmas plus another thousand)

access to the boat is simple to control
which is why it's the only way to get there

47.

this phrase of Aristole's (again) could serve
as shop sign for the life of the anthonite
Beatitudes over and above all things
a vocation to God is contemplative
and amid all the possible vocations
the one that is most blissful is the one that
most faithfully approximates this divine
vocation
        about two thousand monks remain
(a thousand seven hundred corrects the guide)
all pray meditate contemplate come and go
in four-wheel drives some of them act like peasants

48.

everything that comes before reason and cries
out without stopping is the innate complaint
it all issues from our bodies from the earth
there John dips his quill into it when he writes
the Apocalypse the very base seem then
at the tip of the nib ink is obscene light

49.

Karyes the nearby town is the capital
of this theocratic republic that here
occupies the Mount Athos peninsula
each of twenty monasteries is present
house and representative a governor

is the Greek State (one changes him as often
as one changes the government that really
makes one laugh) admission to the Mount was first
decreed by the emperor of Byzantium
Constantine Monomachos in one thousand
sixty the number of monasteries were
limited to the twenty founded from the
tenth to twelth century other foundations
were all then joined to each one of these twenty
dispersed along the coasts and then fortified
like some of those Tibetan castles our skete
was therefore a vassal in spite of its size
fifteen chapels cubicles by the hundreds
apartments studios and kilometers of
corridors subterranean staircases
without speaking of the grand Russian style church
of the central courtyard and the Greek building
that has on its uppermost floor a chapel
where every day John makes a sign to the light
while in the meantime I touch with my eyes skin
the color of whitewashed earth and antique rose

50.

in principle language is ready to think
everything that you seek to think with it but
there's something else about it that has you think
according to furrows impervious tracked
one would say boosting momentum and these are
old commandments the language seems similar
to the lover in the process of finding
what love is with you when really it's crippled
by too much knowledge and by ready made truths

51.

the first thing one sees is a machine of stone
marble canopy that bears at its tympan
the X of Saint Andrew patron of the skete
what's more his head is sculpted at the center
in a medallion on the X of the door
beneath covered in decorative bronzes
then one realizes that this thick metal
could withstand any ordinary attack
is as much solid as any fortress door
to the right at the far end of the building
another perpendicular structure and
in the same style a sign posted facing front
ANTHONIAS in large capital letters
crushes a bit the precision it masters
clerical education Nico explains
seventy childs here and that he took part in
the memory doesn't appear unpleasant
and he becomes visibly very happy
beginning with the word *games* that gives rise to
gestures accompanied by *broken, broken*
suggesting fine ransacking and plundering
from the period when the skete was neglected

52.

Father Maximos' confidences: I gradually formed an
opinion from the accounts of some very old monks.
Toward the end, there remained only three of four old
men here, but it was still a Russian monastery. And
what is Russian remains so in the eyes of the Russians.
So I think that the Russians . . . emptied the monas-
tery of its precious works because they considered them
Russian.—But which Russians? I asked myself telling

myself that a clandestine landing was something quite
difficult.—The Russians from here of course, because
they didn't doubt that the Russian objects were theirs
by right. So they stole them. After which they insti-
gated the great fire of 1958 to conceal the robbery.
in all the things said by Maximos I like
the simple conviction and natural fervor
that always tempers and puts candor in it
his faith similar to telluric forces
overthrows the obstacle or dissolves it

53.

crushed neck the eagle with two heads is rubble
among rubble but the imperial A
still adorns its keel A for Alexander
a tsar thrown so low then reduced to powder
having to have just a historical death
throughout debris destruction great disaster
owing to the force of time and to kids' games
level with the floor crawl linens that crackle
under footsteps the calcified little waves
here and there a pile of disintegrated
rags a load of cotton and limp bandages
and it could be that the last one dead is here
below but what good is looking for a corpse
a particular corpse in the vast carcass
that is today the Empire an iron
door opened with great effort hiding a room
a punctured ceiling a cupboard with twelve doors
liturgical clothing reduced to a pulp
covers the whole floor a magma a batter
with lumps of embroidered crosses that make signs
in the twisted folds the remnants of a stole
armfuls of silk that were trampled underfoot

some pieces of wood some ancient bindings are
planted there like teeth that one suddenly has
extracted from the mastication of time
large drawers similar to lower jawbones
where all this regurgitation overflows
moldy skein of muscle of lacerated
tissues taken apart with pliers and claws
that's how the thing appears to the passerby
which has no name in any language

                                        one must
look at this hole in the center of the head
it's a well from which only silence rises
every creative act fights against the self
wants to create a prolongation of life
while destroying in oneself one's own demise
and that it never seems to end this ending
the new community has already now
recovered a corridor twelve single doors
two double doors opening on two large rooms
offices places to read and reception
the single doors open out to cubicles
two have become kitchen and refectory
one is toilet and shower the nine others
have recovered the function they always had

54.

the novice theologian unearthed for me
cellars and basements some hundred meters crossed
with barrels as sizable as a cabin
saw the enormous machine that was a mill
as well as incinerated beams hanging
from iron wheels twisted stems some broken hoists
this beneath the library that was burned
walked along the corridors where passed the fire
real ovens with red and white walls broken bricks

where every step strikes the lighter creates sparks
no more flames the skin of stones are in ashes
room furnished with piles of rubble another
with piles of scrap metal picks and pickaxes
hammers levers another with curious
drums that have crank handles and stacks of dishes
another with a hundred wooden chair legs
I used to demolish things said the student
coming to a stop in front of a glass ball
me I pick up objects and classify them
on one side small cruets jars inkwells bottles
demijohns most of them fashioned from blown glass
on the other wood tools stools benches a grate
to wash the laundry and that which in Aubrac
we then called "maluque" an enormous wooden
hammer then father Paul gathers together
all the icons and all of the images
portraits of the tsar and tsarina chromos
lithographs from Moscow and from Paris from
Istanbul from Saint Petersburg from London
a city in flames set down on top of this
and it is to my surprise not Moscow that
commits suicide to chase Napoleon
but the famous engraving in red and black
where one sees flames of revenge burn in Paris
that at monuments drove out the pétroleuses
who the devil brought this image to this place
a skull of the osteophylakion
did it contain the thought of a communard

55.

in the sky white mist at sunrise the mist is
pink at sundown where Venus marks the highest
the shadow mouth has eaten Saint John and me
chased out by the darkness of the Greek chapel

I am alone on the planks of the footbridge
I wait for the end another beginning
the White a gray apparition fringed with froth
great silence everywhere then a cricket scrapes
its rattle no thoughts now just the presence of
the present suddenly a rolling downpour
in the nearby mountain torrents of air
that are not more than a breeze arriving here
three stars turn up and I furnish them with names
they are for a fact the paws of the Great Bear
a faint light grows at the back side of the church
my face awaits for the floodtide with fervor
O! that my eyes can soak in this passing life
and that this moon be the one to astonish
which draws the body to the edge of the name
a thousand stars right now and the blue blackens
it looks like the deepest one is surfacing
and puts on it that which it kept underneath
the moon is hidden behind a cupola
the cornice is causing the light to refract
the way a stone does under running water
the flat tint of the planks is a velvet heat
I stretch out on top nape of the neck set down
on a piece of marble and sleepiness comes
when the full moon does perforate my eyelids
it's in the middle of the sky it's a point
a gold wheel eye at the summit of the White
so who moon or rock brings forth the white aura

THE REST OF THE VOYAGE

June 95–June 97

Dresden

walked alongside the Elbe while thinking of you
small sun under overcast skies an old sky
and life is put on edge by a sick tooth seen
at the Albertinum the hand its caress
its youthful gesture trembles by the blue edge
Klinger put the eye to the rock and Corinth
puts sex in your eyes and discovers Slevogt
bought one or two ruins and a taste for time
cannot tell the most beautiful the love games
of a satyr and marble hermaphrodite
they are all naked in the tomb of my mind

∽

porcelain chimes and the rain someone thinks of
the garden that is still forbidden surprised
that it is me in me that I am the one
in the air the chords of a heart to heart choir
wheels furiously stirring the water on streets
think about the secret movement of the curve
that offers and strips all the fleece in oneself
what is the materiality of flesh
and that thing in it that physicality
all substance at this instant unthinkable
when there is a current of form and presence
a fleshy thing that remains without features

∽

Sunday an admiring crowd at the feet of
the Sistine Madonna a real exclusive
where two little rogue angels take center stage
and Rubens chuckles and makes his Leda come
in the beautiful slant of light a bit of
trembling wing little scared Ganymede pisses
all those nudging elbows and those knowing smiles
it makes one forget it's Rembrandt and culture
Saskia wears her hat like she wears her own youth
winking eternally to those passing by
then going out into the night rose in hand
here she is lustrous and gleaming in love's dew
little further off bathed in silence and light
profile leaning toward the paper of her life
is she woman or Vermeer or THE painting
suddenly in the open shutters something
a flash of something unknown you go toward it
a reflection where lowered eyes look at you
from the other side of image and of time
I wait for the void where sight is washed again
brusque that ballet of organs and destiny
and the day is all of a sudden garish

Nowhere 1

no one placed their hands on the nape of my neck
so this way this absence doesn't have a face
it is simply there like a cold sensation
a reminder of that perfect solitude

Struga

what is the poetry of languages hurled
from the top of a bridge three rows of flapping
mouths open wide the night and jets of white light
a few little sparks on the tips of young girls
a torrent bordered by branches brews the air
the flares at festivities where words explode
firecrackers are flung farther than their range
a metamorphosis of verbal matter
where a Pentecost takes place in every ear
the same backwash of emotive eloquence
from the head to the heart sound turns into sense

Popova Sapka

in a street of Terovo the word AME
amid the letters of the unknown language
then up there in the mountain a mistiness
a haze or cloud or the covering of time
on gritty skin and the body caught a chill
from the earth with its green coat to thoughts of snow
that falls gently in the way age comes for us
sight slips now from beauty to bewilderment
while the bus veers to the edge of the shoulder
suddenly a shadow or feeling empty
the depths of the world is it really that deep
I no longer have the taste for literature
asserts someone it is the truth that I need

Poitiers

time has eaten away the stone Adam and
Eve faceless continue facing each other
the tree is now the same as the skeleton
the bicephalous monster has kept its tongues
licks from the tips of its eyes a remnant of
childhood the first garden won't grow back again
hell is always there adjacent to the heart
under painted pillars one tramples the dead
their nothingness covered by a marble page
where the names on these are skeletons of air
the gaze returns back to it like a black breath
taking flight wholly on tiny spirit dust
alongside the walls where pictures perspire
an old Roman chorus thrilled with the Gothic
appears just as obscure as the shadow mouth
where the backlighting produces holes and teeth
time's cry gathers itself at the body's core

TGV

air steams borders leafless branches a low sky
makes eyes believe finally they see matter
what is the space between these open fingers
a steeple nails the view point of history
forest then green wheat a residue of sun
a handful of cows positioned like white stones
there's a bridge an orchard a precocious lamp
day hesitates to let go of the world's frame
it must hang already on that other side
an old sheet returned from too many passions
slowing down helps one discover gentians
a copse on an embankment dappled in red
two idiots in ties talk of added costs
of man's interface before-seeing-must-see
horizon turn blue to give itself to night
a luminous punch puncturing the moment
the black vapor and play at divine splendor
there is there a kind of maddening beauty
and something at the end like a final gift
when life withdraws by letting evaporate
the pinch of nothing that gave it its savor

Marseille

a touch of rose at the level of rooftops
old water buried under little white boats
a thousand masts scrape against a looming sky
to the left the galleys to the right Pouillon
the weather breaks between the two you would like
to pick up invisible debris and see
the present play the same game that images
play in the head climbing back up the black pit
while a bit of rain seeks to moisten eyelids
which turn the gaze and roll it into the sea
whose waves beat beside the pile of vertebrae

La Ferté-Macé

upright granite and beautiful in gray air
a gust of wind twists the breath at the tip of
the tongue first exhibition Jean-Pierre Brisset
prince of budding ideas and unshakeable
logician of these fresh verbal sound systems
nothing remains now of his demonstration
but a silence where winter takes its first steps
a passerby closes the old knife without
handle speculates as to who stole the blade

Naples

tiny pasta in a lentil purée then
friarielli a local herb flavored
with a bitter liquid in which the spicy
contradicts the sweet of the word on the tongue
a city barely glimpsed is an aroma
of images where the steep gardens make faults
amongst the colored terracing of the streets
no other cited place stands similarly
it compresses time under the golden stone
the yellow and the red that colors its walls
history is here eternally present
all eyes stand facing you look at you make that
we always walk in the middle of the view

Who knows what the Chateau de l'Oeuf incubates
its walls protect the delicate shell that one
need only to break to ruin the city
the passerby dreams that this never seen egg
is the eye torn from the Cyclops and kept in
the deepest bottommost in a bath of tears
all the streets are paved with slabs of lava this
way everyone can trample the volcano
it's acting dead this morning under a cloud
lest it suddenly opt not to play porte-ciel
a few palms that make one think of giraffes' necks
drawing out curtsies at the core of the view
everywhere gestures trace in air traces of
arabesques and tendrils in Baroque ceilings
and the waves on the surface of the ocean

Cumae

the sibyl had a brothel for the sailors
and prophesized her girls gave the blow by blow
Jean-Noël says in front of Lake Avernus
the water smells like sulphur or a near hell
it's a black mirror that the moon fades into
perhaps it has giant's blood for silvering
perhaps the smoke of the Phlegraean Fields
ignited the gods to save Mount Olympus
the sea a little further off brews statues
a whole city sunk at the bottom of blue

Pompeii

beauty abolishes time and therefore death
yet still it is made here of one and the same
peculiar mix where life is no longer life
we've only resuscitated destruction
the last inhabitants have plaster bodies
they forever beckon with signs of their end
why have them set down in a cage behind glass
their patience at present equal to that of
the volcano heavy on the horizon
what's the use imagining a chariot's wheels
being stuck in a rut or the game of love
looking at the alcove and the bed of stone
the sky hasn't changed neither has the movement
of cats making themselves a place in the sun

∽

this ruin represents what is eternal
for this reason it can't keep on perishing
it is resurrected from its own ashes
and all those stumps of wall planted in the earth
make jaws in the ground where the wind comes to laugh
unless gods of bygone days didn't by chance
drop the lower half of their mouths refusing
once here to explain the inexplicable
the return of chaos and of the senseless
as if the divine had never taken place

∽

a two-fold painted gesture the mystery
who is the angel flourishing a whip and
the woman coat fallen the little reader
the gaze all excited touching the unknown
to sense there a meaning it can't fix on
it is taken by the harshness of this red
gets to the heart of it still just doesn't get
what it is in him that disrobes him this way

Paris-Nantes

successive rows of shrubs hills and fog curtains
drawn during the entire trip toward Le Mans
current events suffocate us let us breathe
they're a placard in the small sun suddenly
fallen on the top of the station's platform
then lowlands and the specter of apple trees
with the return of the fog fields of dead grass
piles of white bags in middle of green pasture
a herd of limousines and a muddy lake
the mind consumes the images and so keeps
quiet this puts into it a light silence
which sometimes is then itself reflected in
order to just grasp the comings and goings
of vision a crowd of trees washing their feet
in a field of gray water covered in mist

Nantes

vapor rises in air where steam clouds the light
long phantoms enveloping the monuments
the tower with red lights all the way up there
poor little balloons that play at being stars
the city is asleep in a white vapor
all of a sudden it wraps around your face
an abundance of air or the breath of time

Angers

a black and white castle makes the difference
darkness of time becomes stone and round towers
passing image less vivid than a visage
what is uniqueness and what is its nature
it is all woven from form and point-of-view
you gaze at the you beneath the head of hair
mortal desire replicates in its nest
midnight heavy in winter covers ardor
the encounter breaks at the edge of the road

Train Corail

but why is it that he failed asks the poster
but why is it that he's dead replies my tongue
which infuriates the living their failure
the earth today is flat to the very end
a light green followed by dark green then the sky
that occasionally falls on heads of trees
in the thickness of windowpanes shadows pass
placing the outside inside or the reverse
the eyes are the place where the same shift occurs

Issoudun

take leave of George Sand then catch up with Balzac
he left behind Zulma's ass while moaning that
for each night of love a novel is ruined
too many pages so far grumbled Musset
who would always prefer a cunt to paper
and playing with the prick instead of the pen
one had the court of law and justice blown up
so there is nothing left now but the ground floor
so it is deprived of its staircase of shame
the thickness of time is very present here
thought is based on it and looks for the angle
where the day thrown open burst forth out into
the great bustle's continual concealment

Forbach

everywhere temples to the old misery
dwellings of pain of waiting of not enough
being human a long task of illusion
the snow and the cold a good little winter
along the many exigencies of hope

TGV

night arrives slow and gray a virus in air
and the gaze looks feeling its vast encroachment
some smoldering three houses a line of snow
how to see the way the picture penetrates
its backward surge when words throw it out of doors
but nothing nothing nothing a round of light
a few lines hardly perceived in all that speed
language is swept up and blown away by time
darkness has already saturated space
each thing is as a result reduced to smoke
solitude stretches out across the window

Aubrac

fog and snow childhood has forgotten its way
a fragment of wet sky blocks the window time
a hole that always constantly moves forward
a trap opened too soon for the last moment
further down winter retires in the light
all that remains is a bit of white moisture
recollections fall from who knows not what tree
with memory breaking all of the branches

Nowhere 2

light in the eye so crude that it cracks the egg
the head is also harrowed by the brightness
oh the glass hammering the nail in the tongue
crown of nettles around the eyes on all sides
no image will be able to wash all that

Lisbon

seven small hills and no pope a wavering
when the colossal sun gnaws the sea of straw
the houses are all lined up like spectators
that remain upright in front of others that
see them age as time hangs its laundry to dry
the city is so splattered with red that from
above one thinks its taken a bloody hit
the eye seeks everywhere the white of legend
but the puny present covered everything
just the body of the poet stayed intact
liquor preserves much better than memory
so do we conceal under a heavy stone
the proof that being is less than non-being
who'll know how to play with intranquility
for endurance to finally stuff the skin
and change appearance into immortal flesh
one instant to the next a new corpse is dead
just as dead as the oldest of all corpses
that strange equality that collapses time

Saint-Étienne

art moves out of its frame to occupy space
these days it bears the name of instillation
a static spectacle which when filled up sees
when the view is an arrested thought a strange
ethereal impression where the narrative
is a visual act the beginning perhaps
of a whole art fusing in the visible
an act of intellectual proportions
this time Prigow Jaccard an undertaking
that ties gestures and ritual to wasting time

Annecy

red eye reverberates back the sun the white
of the stone becomes completely violet
air suddenly crushes and creases the lake
night walks very gently on top of this sight
Ménetou Salon brandades magret rosé
and friendship isn't afraid of saying things
outraged at being sniffed by a dog this way
the swan tries to bite it with some dignity
never know who could've put time on a stake
the ducks thrash the water because it is black

Nowhere 3

live flesh thrown into that precise moment heart
blazing the head burns its rags of memory
smoke takes to the sky and plays at being clouds
here there at the tip of the eyes embracing
a pure movement to return the you to you

Fonteluco

silence has ripened in the same way the rocks
a crust and underneath there's the same substance
from surface to the bottom nothing changes
the gaze investigates in vain space and time
and beauty is confused with what's obvious
the broom trees over there put gold in the air
and thinking here puts a dagger in the head
papers butchered everywhere the flesh open
a continuous cry ploughs into the skin

Florence

the present as always makes war on the past
no hand-to-hand combat but skillful treason
beauty presented for the eyes appetite
serves to mask a long-drawn-out execution
one sells this spectacle speaking of culture
each of us must dress oneself in solitude
for presence to obliterate the present

San Galgano

here the limit indicates an opening
infinity unveiled from the beginning
time becoming form has done away with time
it is at present music made visible
on the wing of who the gaze becomes angel

Champdieu

the proportions at times prompt the sky to think
the garden therefore is in the open head
to look is to see the interior view
the long fold stirs according to the hidden
which comes to the edge of form a white shadow
the boxwood knows that better than us it builds
by ardor of the line springboards for the eye
the infinite sets itself thus within reach
the tree is always of life or of knowledge
from the moment where the sap of breath appears
it isn't important to have a green thumb
but to be able to bring through the branches
this flowering of air that we call being

Verona

graffiti more lovely than the balcony
but it's what dictates desire for duration
as if two names interlaced in the plaster
could perhaps similarly dominate time
the city lives a love where the whole of life
is an ancient dream always re-inspired
one sells by the millions Juliet's kisses
yet not even in sugar language Shakespeare

Perillos

there are fog flowers in the river of air
bit by bit they cover the entire view
space is satiated by the mist of time

Pas de l'As

a heart beats inside the wood of the door where
dates names listed persons from another time
in the cavity of these signs a vague life
you come to a stop on the black rock and see
the curve where the sky already touched the earth

Nevers

a chill hangs in the air causing one to dream
of intense kisses in some very old rooms
here and there the past lives on in what remains
but the pavements towers beautiful high walls
are prey to the ugliness of the present
the Niève river is buried in all these pipes
and to top it all the cultural flagstone
death's moreover the glory of the city
ever since the mayor past prime minister
thought suicide the socialist betrayal
killing himself a first of May on the bank
where dogs go straddle each other and lovers
whereas the president who picked at his soul
gave all of his books to the library so
that one could come study their dedications

Lyon

the old and new marry at the opera
every night rose juice surges from the rooftop
the you walks from river to river watches
the smoke of the present rise up on the Croix-
Rousse he remembers thinks of Philippe Soupault
eating some chocolate as well as puss-in-boots
who was eating his stomach while laughing death
has conceptualized their two faces at
the same time as La Place des Terreux remains
the chocolates the water inexhaustible
and the same red sky constantly becoming

Madison

the air gray like the walls of the capitol
unless the two lakes lost their color on it
the city waits for snow and me some childhood
a part of the passing season in the wind
time scrapes at the heart and the back of the eyes
suddenly body buried in old laundry
near there a youth passes by on bicycle
during the time when the squirrels do the garbage
Steve drives me toward the tower of Babel there
eleven young ladies study my language
their own waits for life under the lure of lips

Chicago

so many highs and lows sharp turns on the wing
that the earth also trembles stands itself up
shaking up its shorelines and its skyscrapers
life leans in and abuts right against the teeth
the head is an unusual sort of stopper
that's badly pushed in the eye seeks a landmark
but streets blocks neighborhoods as much as graveyards
align infinitely our human death then
the present sews the day back up under wheels
the number letter obsess the passerby
returned therefore all the countless to crying
to the unknown face that hinges on the next
day-to-day back-beat beating of the eyelash

Niagara

passing the bridge the vapors draw near to us
blue pipes white smokestacks steel walls and the river
is favorable to the slumber of birds
fashioning lines of black dots on green water
then abruptly the surface is less massive
sunken crests and the eddies churn the thickness
murmurs rolling contrary to the current
make the air hoarse and rouses in the viewing
a rumbling racket and perdition of sense
all folds pay lip service to abyss and falls
explodes at bottom where pulverized ascends
again vapor volcanoes blowing great clouds
that send chills down the spine of this little life

Miami

it's the business district that scrapes at the sky
money laundered at the edge of blue water
everywhere else the city is flat pastel
thousands of times given to water's embrace
coconut trees palms nothing much else is left
but paradise has no need for trees seeing
that for all consuming some sun suffices
you watch to see the large ocean liners pass
amid the houses covered by their shadows

Houston

a million inhabitants in just eight years
that then makes four so the city is the fourth
and yet there's still open country everywhere
green oaks boxwood thickets and azaleas
and gardens with red cardinals and blue jays
but no strolling passers-by just a few dust
blowers and leaf removal machines that help
move for nothing a few clouds above the ground
there's free admission to the Rothko Chapel
little shop of silence and forgetfulness
where sight brightens by gazing at surfaces
mirroring what stirs deep inside the body
black is the only interior color
the one wise thing is to make a door of it

Cholula

raised the Virgin on the back of the Devil
in the distance the volcano hurls some smoke
white cloud that covers over the sky with haze
that is how the ancient gods handle the word
mist around the deepest parts of memory
where the wounds and the blood of Christ are painted
the soul likewise adorns itself with prayer
in this place truth is a firework display
or a countenance given crudely to grief
pilgrim bicyclists pass by very quickly
in a sound of fabric crumpled with two hands

Puebla

the cathedral is closed as is its courtyard
God is finally on strike for the first time
history strings together fatigued facades
that are paved with black stones and disfigured walls
that which keeps enduring is a chocolate sauce

Teotihuacan

it's here in this place that gods are created
the name keeps this assertion in the present
one senses everywhere a fallow presence
coming from monuments that fashion in air
who knows what possible arrangements of space
of geometry from which these forms ascend
to look at the serpent is so much simpler
the feathered beast flies out of a corolla
but this god of stone and history is a lure
stops us from hearing the voices of the dead
everything it says has already been said
it has amnesia sing under peoples steps
a murmur nonetheless rolls its noisy bones
and heard at all levels of the pyramids
in the effort of climbing up toward the top
one senses once there how much it alone is
able to harmonize the living and dead

Chichen Itza

the pelota players are inside the rock
therefore killing the conqueror has no end
his blood causes flowers and snakes to spring forth
a tree establishes its roots in a jaw
on that terrain we gained only to die in
there are shields and masks and jaguars everywhere
what a laugh to see our life so very small
the Tzompantli is a wall that is sculpted
one part of it stone and several rows of skulls
where sacrificial heads were exhibited
further off eagles eat away human hearts
the Sun god liked feeding himself the same way
and what did Venus make of this clawed monster
all adorned with his feathers in lieu of love
his temple a pile of ruins and regrets
to climb to the summit of the pyramid
better go barefoot than in slippery soles
though vertigo awaits you on the way down
not too much risk for the pleasure of seeing
space tip over into the hollow of time
what did the one thousand and one pillars serve
raised up on terraces and biting blue air
the uppermost ones demarcate a market
that we reached via a colossal staircase
at the center an impluvium and in
the gaze the desire that the passenger
come to an end silence and harmony at
the edge of being the Chichanchob and its
phallic figure further off but a shelter
of questions too calm in their statue slumber
the gods no longer insist on blood or hearts
one would willingly offer them either one

to stop Caracol from becoming Babel
but once more the place celestial bodies speak
ruined then the temple of obscure writing
ruined is that of the Initial Series
ruined even the ruin of old knowledge
its mastery of the universe by form
where a few red hands mackle the memory
and put onto its wall a sign that says NO

Tulum

in ceasing to exist gods create in air
an emptiness where the light comes to settle
all their monuments gather around the edge
the earth underneath congeals its ancient waves
see the god descending from a pediment
he was supposed to induce the rain's downfall
it's the sky today that drops into the rock
to very gingerly liberate our heart
and elongate the view toward the end of time
same at its core to the Caribbean Sea
its green water took the divine in its folds
all then ends up in rumbling and murmuring
all began in an identical manner

Coba

forest forest the road between two green walls
coconut palms rubber plants and unknown ones
intersected an iguana on tiptoe
a directory thrown open on the road
and three Mayan pueblos where on the ropes dry
embroidered dresses and blouses products of
some academy of the craft industry
seeks the destruction of native inventions
also stationed everywhere temple tradesmen
offering everyone the same cheap rubbish
the forest of Coba devours the site
one sees trees in the process of eating rock
roots all around the rocks forming a stomach
the pyramid is a pouring of blocks piles
of human vertebrae like a skeleton
the ancient order is at present lost time
the way that goes astray here at *contre-ciel*

Jerusalem

a large sun puts some blood on the horizon
the city beneath is smeared over with chalk
too many new districts overpower hills
their aim is to chase history from the present
but the skin of the earth is hard and its heart
beats all the more so that one wants to crush it
in the ancient city one tramples on time
blowing in ones face a ingenuous soul
a few blue flags fly their insult in the air
of the district whose point it's to belittle
even so life doesn't lessen its boiling
on cobblestones where the man of the cross passed
how to colonize what belongs to being
when one has the willingness only to have

Helsinki

lakes in every corner are parts of the sea
a bit of a breeze forever skims the light
that passes through the legs of passing women
white lilacs purple lilacs and wet weather
one seeks at midnight a name for the brightness
when the sun rolls itself about in the flour
a cotton sky makes the wings inaudible
while sunset shakes at the bottom of water
the houses of God and house of the People
perpetuate their confrontation with bells
and Saarinen and Aalto compete
one has got the shoulder the other the square
but love goes toward the curve not toward the angle
nature has left behind some trees and some rocks
shadow gardens and handsome mounds of granite
that arch their backs in the center of these lawns
some large boats smoke and eat away in silence
lines of motor vehicles and visitors
an ice-breaker waits now for the white season

THE REST OF THE POEM

1.

premonitions faded rags tatters of soul
vapor of vapors bursting forth in the brain
a whole dross of complaints finally done in
a gesture loiters nearby that wants some sky
to catch the intelligible and kill it

2.

we call all our ruins reminiscences
syllables made of sand and these first names where
the alphabet comes to lay an obscure need

3.

the you looks at its silence and how to live
everything at once being and non-being

4.

the body always an incomplete present
its very unity strays in its own depths
in the mass of meat its continuity
all organic places are passing places
flux reflux throbbing palpitations movements
and life is never the same in the same place
it is a gust of wind that goes through the flesh
bones signal are defeated by this breathing
a phrase in us white and undecipherable

5.

the man looks he gives in this way to the space
his own form without even realizing
so that he falls back into his heaviness
his head and heart well covered by his big me

6.

bit of air and suddenly heavy fatigue
why don't we have replacements for the body
and an array of organs to barter with

7.

when life then takes back that which belongs to it
there remains nothing of each but an image
this bit of smoke the guarantee of being

8.

where does bias toward identity come from
a cigarette between these fingers of thought
yearning of yesteryears drowned in saliva
a vague frost around the nerves where it came from

9.

no circles at the surface of silence just
a darkness that thickens whenever one bends
and at the far back a complete *contre-ciel*

10.

a solitude where the language licks itself

11.

the dead observe each one of us die they smile
at our awkwardness toward metamorphosis
they have hindsight are already used to it

12.

what's the point covering oneself with a house
when life always seems to flow under the door
someone laps up the waves on the other side
a small sound the same one to the very end

13.

feel the step of time on the skin of the eyes
over there bones are making signs dry and white
then the day rises at the end of blue lips
a verbal dewy moistening of the place
syllable syllable which could say it all
and instead it only makes folds on the tongue
we have again brushed against the solution

14.

why then is knowledge a constraint to language
or else a poor coin in the hand of the dead

15.

make of me what I am cries out desire
but time's nothing but a cluster of minutes
too much twilight and this delta of sexes
one can't always fraternize with nothingness
even if azure skies run into the gaze

16.

how to excavate the flesh with this dagger
the blade is illusory the handle too
and its aim is itself not that different
the mental tool searches in vain the sharp edge

17.

the known serves as a measure for the unknown
this is why the mystery remains intact
the mouths of the dead did not perish with them

18.

a ball of sound a fictitious festival
the heads we didn't carry on our shoulders
have now come one by one to occupy ours
with their five senses and their severed ideas
their way of tossing the obscure in the O

19.

all of this plants a firebrand in our throat
nothing survives it except a few embers
we catch our death warming ourselves up in them

20.

we already counted the steps the distance
phrases needed to sacrifice to the dogs
language that we will restore to the serpent
what's the use of the tick-tock of rhetoric
it cares only for its own perpetuance
its old appetite eats away at our hearts
and it will rise up to our face a flushing

21.

ah at last the sun is sent to the corner

22.

life doesn't ever hold up inside a life
but what are I and you what secrets tie them
to the same linen tatters of flesh and skin
history's a pile of moth-eaten laundry
we will save from it nothing but the stitches

23.

we dream in a contretemps of nudity
that it has visual corporeality
like a fruit of air hung to the tree of life

24.

paper forest burns at the ends of the earth
columns of letters escape the sinister
the alphabet calculates the survivors
and too bad for the gods and their little paws
creating beauty on the palms of the rocks

25.

we know well that we must refresh the usage
change the value as much as the point of view
the flesh considered for its composition
will become industrial material
one must re-see the social the cultural
scour the framework and give it a cold stare
enough of this waste we count the syllables

26.

a donkey's jawbone and the sound of a blow
the beginning was already worth the end
with all this blood that was flowing in the source
time folds up on top of all this a first shroud
a fist-full of earth falls down onto the mouth

27.

no more vertebrae there's a column of words
with at the summit a flutter of meaning
the page is an eyelid where he falls asleep
his waking the accident or alibi
which makes of the reader then a prince charming

28.

a syllable that shatters and is reborn
a mini maybe its strand of desire
makes for a lean sound in the depths of the flesh

29.

memory is a hand deprived of fingers
its ungainliness terrifies the future

30.

the value of the body always dropping
everywhere one makes more of it than one should
one would need to draw out human energy
oh what pills the future could then be given
raising again the value of the human
then the extract would be worth many bodies

31.

all injury must eat away at its pain
apart from that what purpose would its form serve

32.

one genesis can hide in it another
the discharge of words doesn't cease to thicken
language's horizon is always behind
the reader's eye turns on the cliff of silence
dying is the denial of illusion
history is a mask placed on top of this
or else who'd sleep on the edge of the black hole

33.

climbed up on top of others a head protrudes
its gaze turns and turns and then it comes toppling
another head climbs upward its eyes shut closed

beautiful balloon stuffed with noisy trinkets
it's forgotten the position of the real
in the end it's only a head full of heads
will it bud therefore like a cauliflower
a bit of reason climbing back up its roots
the vague souvenir of a human image
what good would it serve one visage more or less
the last head is the one that falls in the heart
a splash disseminates terror in the flesh
in the middle of all these vowels crashing
another head perseveres up toward the top
so as to contemplate the whole disaster

NOTES

Introduction

page xi:

Epigraph: "The body is a quarry for words and its explorers assure that there, under the skin, is enough to remake the language." Bernard Noël, http://www.etonnants-voyageurs.net/spip.php?page=invites&id_article=5213

Algerian militants of the FNL: National Liberation Front

his horror of hypocrisy and bad faith that pervaded that period in France: *Bernard Noël: le corps du verbe*, ENS éditions, 2008.

page xii:

liberated him from an internal censure: "Entretien avec Bernard Noël," propos recueillis par Jacques Ancet, http://pretexte.perso.neuf.fr/PretexteEditeur/ancien-site/revue/entretiens/entretiens_fr/entretiens/bernard-noel.htm

write it as a dictionary: Bernard Noël from a letter to Serge Fauchereau, 1984, in *Bernard Noël* by Hervé Carn, Seghers, 1986.

"Passing Mount Athos": "Le Passant de l'Athos," *passant* from the verb "to pass," which in French immediately calls to mind Baudelaire's famous poem "À une passante" ("To a Woman Passing By").

rhythm can be applied to a whole other container: *L'Espace du poème, Entretiens avec Dominique Sampiero*, P.O.L., 1998.

"défi de l'impair!" (challenge of the irregular!"): Ibid.

page xiii:
("Something that would be a strong constraint and invisible like a monastic rule."): Ibid.

page xv:
(All oeuvre is what it is . . . a trace): Ibid.

page xvi:
a reading we gave in Paris: The reading with Bernard Noël and myself can be heard at:
http://doublechange.org/2010/10/08/25-10-10-bernard-noel-elena-rivera/
he says in the interview: En Présence, entretien conduit par Jean-Luc Bayard, L'Amourier éditions, 2008.
"tout est: 'Work-in-progress' jusqu'au bout.": "Everything is: 'Work-in-Progress' up to the end." *En Présence*, entretien conduit par Jean-Luc Bayard, L'Amourier éditions, 2008.
will culture become our lost paradise?: Ibid.
distinguish the visible from the real: Ibid.

page xvii:
"one must make an effort toward the other": Ibid.

NOTES TO THE POEMS

Passing Mount Athos

9.
daddy: In English.
our skete: Bernard Noël lived in Saint-André, one of the "sketes" or "monastic communities" on Mount Athos.

19.

skullotheque: In French, *crânothèque* plays with the sound of *biblio-thèque,* the word for library.

23.

the one Fracasse: *Le Capitaine Fracasse* is a novel by Théophile Gautier published in 1863.

31.

except in an act like Mallarmé's: On September 8, 1898, Mallarmé woke up suffocating; he died the next morning from a spasm of the glottis.

32.

the moon plays the game of the frog and the ox: "The Ox and the Frog" is a small poem by Jean de La Fontaine. A frog wished to be as big as the Ox and exploded in the process. An earlier version of the story was told in Aesop's *Fables.*

46.

a Diamonitirion or Stamped Letter / from the Surveillance Sacrée: Government letter with official stamp.

51.

clerical education: In English.
seventy childs here: [sic] In English.
the word *games*: In English.
broken, broken: In English.

54.

pétroleuses: female fire-raisers during the commune of 1871. Accused of burning down much of Paris at the time but actually didn't.
osteophylakion: Greek word. A place where one conserves bones.
communard: a supporter of the Paris Commune.

55.

the shadow mouth: Refers to Victor Hugo's poem: "Ce que dit la bouche d'ombre."

The Rest of the Voyage

"Popova Sapka":
AME: Abr. "accord monétaire européen," also the word for "soul."

"Annecy":
Ménetou Salon: A type of wine.
brandades: Pounded salt cod mixed with garlic, oil, and cream.
magret rosé: Pink fillet (of duck).

"Verona":
one sells by the millions Juliet's kisses: Reference to cakes sold in Verona called "Juliet's Kisses."

"Pas de l'As":
A place in Aubrac. Land that belonged to the author's family. It is placed where it's *passé à l'as*, "down the drain."

"Lyon":
puss-in-boots / who was eating his stomach while laughing: The story whereby Puss-in-Boots tricks the ogre into turning into a mouse and eats him.

The Rest of the Poem

9.

and at the far back a finished contre-ciel: *Le contre-ciel* ("the counter-heaven" or "anti-sky") is the title of a book by René Daumal.

26.

a donkey's jawbone and the sound of a blow: Judges 15:13-17: The hero Samson slays one thousand men with the jawbone of an ass.

ACKNOWLEDGMENTS

Some versions of some of these translations first appeared in *Denver Quarterly, Eleven Eleven, Web Conjunctions, Tuesday; An Art Project, Tarpaulin Sky, Circumference: Poetry in Translation,* and the *Nation.*

The translator wishes to thank the National Endowment for the Arts, the Santa Fe Art Institute for awarding her the Witter Bynner Poetry Translator Residency, and the Fundacíon Valparaíso in Mojácar, Spain.

The translator is also grateful to Bernard Noël for his generosity and help, along with the invaluable help and support of Olivier Brossard, Denise Newman, Russell Switzer, Susan Stewart, and to Keith and Rosemarie Waldrop for their support and help with the cover.

BERNARD NOËL is a poet, novelist, essayist, historian, and art critic. He received the Prix National de Poésie in 1992 and was given the poet laureateship as well as the Grand Prix International Guillevic-Ville de Saint-Malo for his oeuvre in 2005. He is the author of numerous books, including: *La Chute des temps* and *Extraits du corps* from Poésie/Gallimard and *Le Reste du voyage: Et Autres Poèmes* from Points/poésie Seuil.

ELÉNA RIVERA is the recipient of a 2010 National Endowment of the Arts Fellowship. Her translation of Isabelle Baladine Howald's *Secret of Breath* was published by Burning Deck Press (2009), and other translations can be found in the *Chicago Review, Circumference, Tarpaulin Sky, Tuesday: An Art Project,* and *Web Conjunctions.* She was awarded the 2007 Witter Bynner Poetry Translator Residency at the Santa Fe Art Institute.

Book design and composition by BookMobile Design and Publishing Services, Minneapolis, Minnesota. Manufactured by Versa Press on acid-free 30 percent postconsumer wastepaper.